THE ALCHEMY OF MELANCHOLY

THE ALCHEMY OF MELANCHOLY

poems and drawings
from a world on fire

KATIE BENN

DK

First American Edition, 2026
Published in the United States by DK Publishing
1745 Broadway, 20th Floor, New York, NY 10019

The authorized representative in the EEA is Dorling Kindersley
Verlag GmbH. Arnulfstr. 124, 80636 Munich, Germany

DK, a Division of Penguin Random House LLC
26 27 28 29 30 10 9 8 7 6 5 4 3 2 1
001-357294-SEP2026

A catalog record for this book
is available from the Library of Congress.
ISBN 979-8-217-14016-9

DK books are available at special discounts when purchased in bulk for sales promotions, premiums, fund-raising, or educational use. For details, contact SpecialSales@dk.com

Printed and bound in China

www.dk.com

MIX
Paper | Supporting responsible forestry
FSC™ C018179

This book was made with Forest Stewardship Council™ certified paper – one small step in DK's commitment to a sustainable future.
Learn more at
www.dk.com/uk/information/sustainability

For the initiates of the Melancholic Order

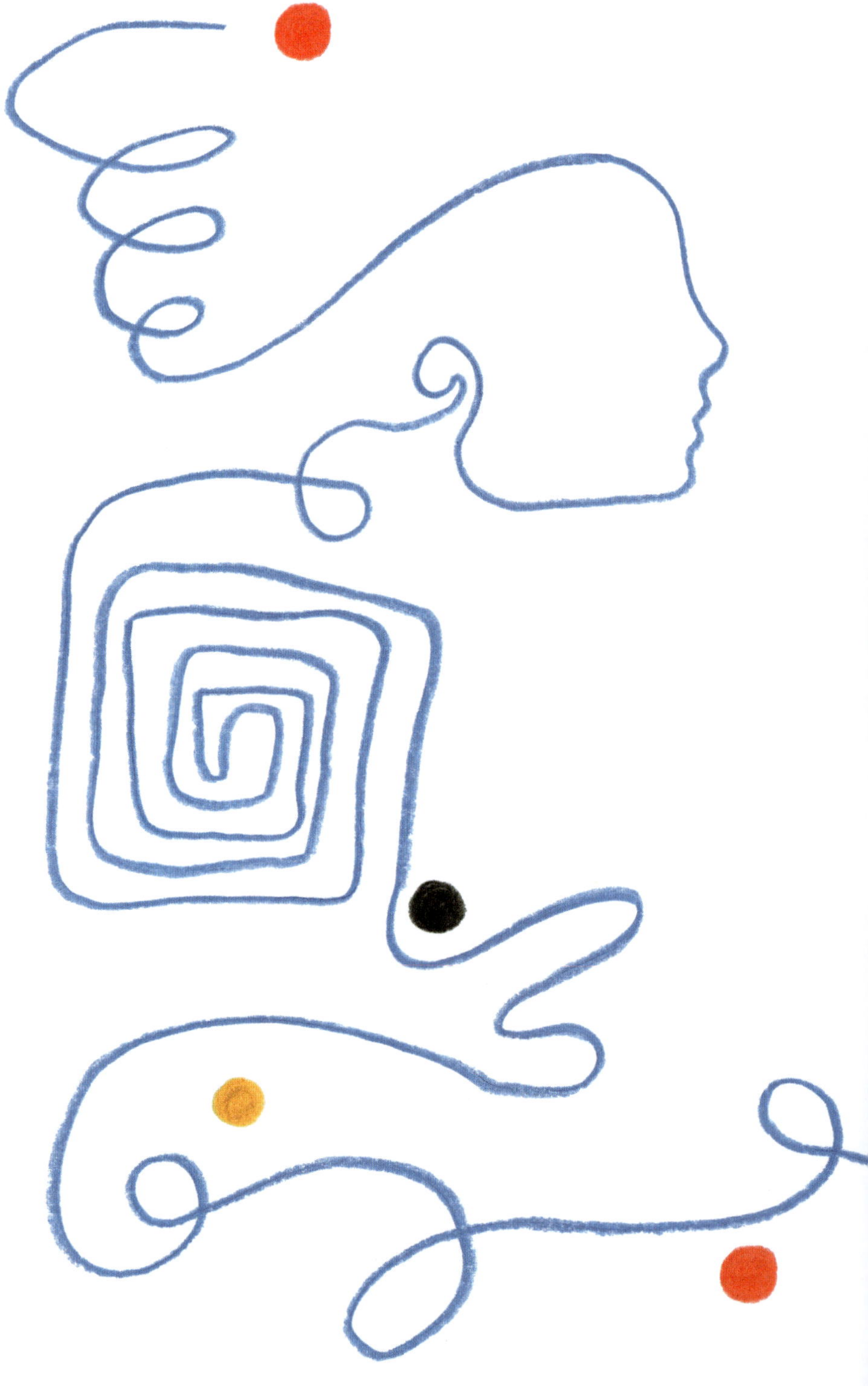

Contents

Prologue

Restless. At each interval,
the curse. We must allow it.
Mercurial, we become like infants
every time, unaware, unsure,
of how to stand upright and speak.

Our new teeth, in due course, cause us to bleed
and worry and tongue what emerges, though
when we are new, we are new—it is plainly this:
nothing suits the new person for a while.

Try not to take it personal; it is a liminal thing.
Undead and somewhat unborn,
the state between two selves is a living ghost,
as new skin comes with time
and our old, outworn hides slink slow into the embers.

Amid such combustions are gigantic ideas
strewn around the head—inductions, contradictions,
notes, meditations—
precious holograms of what might bring happiness,
lightbulbs that enlighten us,
and from other counterintuitive remarkable ages,
they can darken the room, pull
both the hair and the air out of the minutes.

The heart, with all its blood,
exposed to the heat of the fire,
becomes no thing but a series of fits
stacked into a shape that looks like us,
and it does not slow down once we've found a way
of living that makes all practical sense.

It is true, the beginnings,
they sprout, straining amid descent—
but future highs are incomplete,
short of lower points where they stretch and spring.

Such is the trip of life;
retrogrades, compressions, unbearable at the outset,
prove often but a portion of a story more complete,
abundant in following chapters with enduring offerings
of newness and antigravity.

When all is seemingly settled, the ensemble is ready,
stomach emptied of the meal, waiting
by the door, poking, rousing with plots—
sturdy promises of all things more grand
if we simply say yes.

PECULIAR EXPLOSIONS
GHOST STORIES
MUSIC

TO BURN

L'appel du Vide

The last wonder of the world.
The Pit—a marvel.
The scientists, schoolchildren, tourists
travel by boat and by plane to see.
Leery, groaning, some camels, too,
wander the droughty flatlands
and tread curious into the crowd.

The elephants, though, stay a field away.
The birds, they fly around it.
The people, they stare, gripping a rail
and a bag of popped corn.
Some man is selling the bags where the line begins
to see The Pit. People love to come
and spit into the void.
They shout "HELL-OOO!" in singsong,
though they aren't there to greet but for their own voices
to bounce around the hole, until they dampen,
get lost in the dark and dissolve.

"What's down there anyway?" the people always ask.
No one will go in,
though its mouth has a breeze and the desert is hot.
A pair of brothers pretend to push each other
over the rail—it is ceremony.

The Omen

Shout my hair quiet. No matter the food,
tastes of a spiked unripe fruit
on the tongue. What time does—
do it to me quick and bold.
I am unknown to my life again.

A warehouse of adaptations

The Little Wish

There will be a rip in time,
and you
will be transported away,
and someone
beside you will be happy to say,
"Welcome back."

They will tilt their head,
take a cursory peek
through the gate from whence you came,
and scoff, appalled—
"I see what you mean."

An ideal portal

How Do You Handle the Cold

Nestled in the stars, big bright baby nebula,
or are you a snow cave filled to the brim
with twenty of you, singing old
songs of springtime and yesterday?

In Lieu of a Plan

Nets to catch better days.
Traps to snap up the good ideas.
Empty buckets lining the front yard.
Naive baby buttercups, petals outstretched,
facing the sky, waiting for the story to change.

If only you could employ new senses
these days, you could feel better
where to place the buckets, the traps,
the snap nets, and catch it all—
put your energy in, strategic
to when and where the weather is right.

Until then, you'll keep your eyes
set out the window,
when your hands aren't dipped in the buckets
sifting, feet kicking the traps,
fingers folded in the nets.

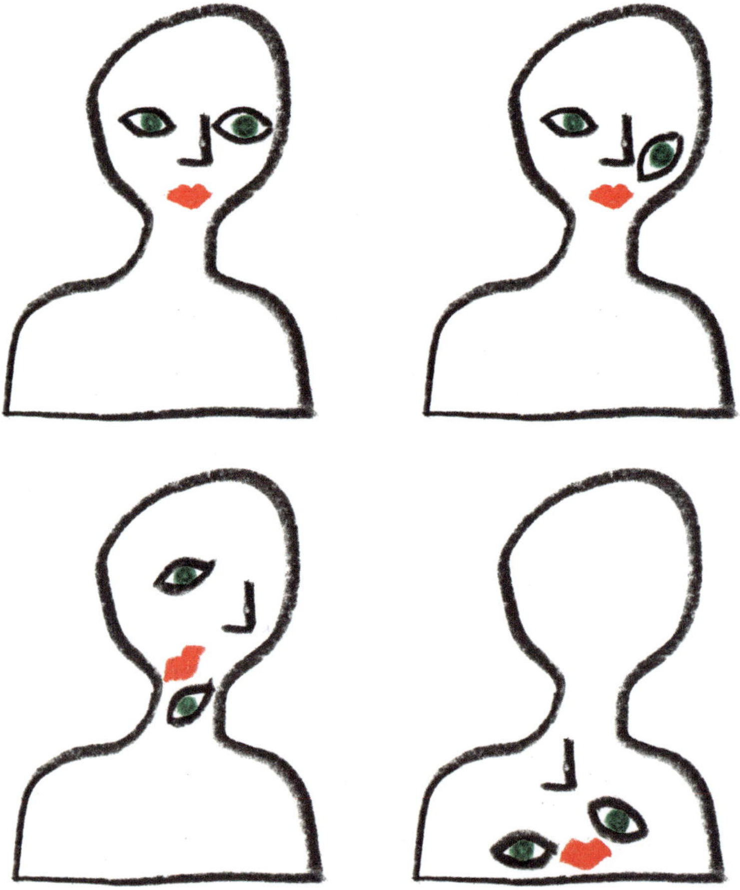

"How have you been?"

Dead Birds Everywhere

We keep doing it—
hold it like it's a bird.
Ten thousand tiny feathers, satin smooth.
Little cool feet, a candied fluttering heart.
Cradled with both hands, carefully
and lightly so as not to squash it,
this humming in a finger cage.
And then as it goes, as if we forget
we are possessing the bird,
taking care of the bird—
distractions come along
and we squeeze.

Clip Your Toenails at Least

What rock is in my bunk?
What demon of dishwasher brain
snores in sea-shanty bars beside me?
Hot sweat through a rusted set of springs.
Hogging blankets, sand in the bed.
Sharp features tearing holes in the threads.
Skin teacher-pupil-apple red.
A cello's f-holes for eyebrows.
Crusted, singed hair and horns.
Impolite as reared by a crown
of tiny tricksy high-fiving flames.
Insomnia, you gloat whilst asleep,
whistling for me in a dream.

The Griever

Woke up at 3am, the tonnage renewed.
A subscription from birth, never growing stale,
undeniably tiresome but never unripe, consistent,
a full sack at a time. You must have noticed.
Always moving in, never fully packing out.

The pale that comes with it enters
from the head, burrows a hole
right in the ribs, makes large rocks of the arms.
Oddly, though, and I can't tell you why—
it does absolutely nothing with the legs.

The inside on the outside, I am a river mouth
emptying into the sea;
my shallow, fragile human person breath,
the lungs, humid-heavy.

Sadness is salt water self-aware, surely
a bit smug. It knows it is also
the line of trees along the muddy road,
and the note in the jacket in the blue hour, saying,
"Yes, old friend. We are doing this again."

Three psychics conjure the color blue

Technically, We Are Lost in Space

Planting seeds, heirlooms
in the indoor garden, heat lamps hot
on high at all times of the day.
Still eating from travel provisions
and the rations are running low,
but the garden should be growing soon,
and I plan to eat from there.

I check the radio once a day, out of habit
tweaking the dials, no one is ever there,
though I heard it wise to leave
a message anyway.

The persistence of the string songs,
music that plays from another room—
or is it in the walls?
I can't describe it; I can never find it.

Enough time unattended, things hum—
operate by themselves, muffled, mumbling.

I haven't found the silver flowers.
No water from the star-dust, storm-dust.
Lost on a rock, I must
make the bed to keep me out of it.

Placing an Ad in the Personals

Help me, come with hands
young, old, tired, or filthy.
Work together, combine
the hands. Place them all around
the eyes. Make a pinhole.
I am trying very hard to see
the thing far away—an outburst
of joy sustained—a shared relief
in the shadow of what
has worked before.
Say yes.
Come today.

Obfuscations

RIGHT?

The Remedy

If I put on the pineapple raincoat first thing in the morning
brush my teeth with baking soda until I'm coughing sparkles
drink only fresh-squeezed juice with fizz
place the orange peel over my teeth and smile in the mirror
mismatch my socks to make them lemon-lime
listen to the star sounds of the plinking celesta
rinky-dink around on the Suzuki Omnichord and hit record
name my houseplants after fruits and greet them each with that name
paint my car to match the melons
and with scented markers, if I draw the two-toned calamansi
this'll all change weight and turn sun-yellow, correct?

RIGHT?

Soft Teeth

I cannot stop chewing on the bones of old joy.
Of warm days, happily unslept, ailing with it.
Chomping, crunching. I can taste it
faint between the teeth, juices numbing the jaw.
Will I only stop when I've chipped every tooth?
There isn't much left of such facile pleasures.
Fruit of frivolity and triumphs from youth;
former fulfillment deep in the marrow;
souvenirs colored by the last remembering.
I can't stop—fracture splinters in the gums.
But what else is there?
Sticky mementos lining the jewelry box;
a xylophone of slippery bones, echoes—
one by one, dulcet and bright with each bite,
but in a short sustain,
growing shorter with each return.

This must be good enough 'til spring,
or else.

Physics of Malaise (The Chair)

If a pile of clothing begins to grow
in the home, you will notice that over time
and in wavelengths, the entropy spreads.
Stretching, expanding in size and strength.
Though this beast of fabric won't touch the walls,
the pictures in frames hung by nail, thumbtack,
or even the sturdiest French cleat, will begin to hang crooked.
A little too left, or all the way to the right,
tilting toward the stitch-sewn hillside
as they begin to link arms with the closet and the bed.

Like plants in distress, releasing chemicals
in unimaginable patterns, pulsing their cry for help,
and the forest bed and its consciousness,
responding with hands made of vine and root,
so are the strewn sweaters, hollering,
the shirts and the pants, woven scarves
and coats, wailing in a frequency
only the surrounding perceived inert can hear.

The spores of disorder tug in all directions.
It is law.

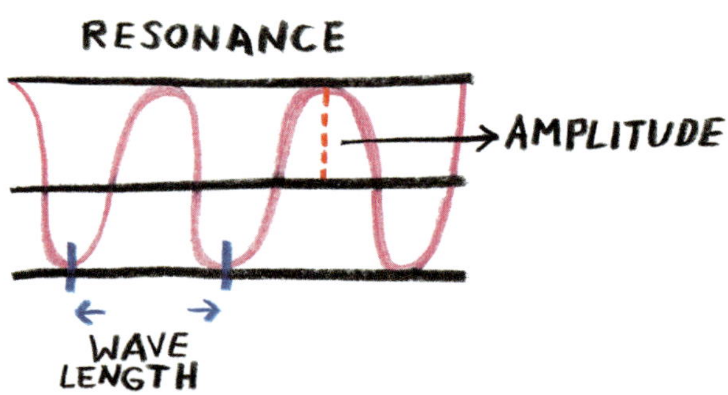

The Hermit, Initially

In the exhibition, put the pamphlet away.
Deposit a quarter and hold the viewer made of resin and glass.
Hold it up to the display cabinet to see
the humongous human model of me.

Move the viewer around; you can spy into my eyes.
I am in there if you squint, a half a mile out
coming to conclusions, questions,
scribbling on a stump.

Pull the viewer across my limbs.
There I am, tiny, walking along the vessels,
doing stand-up for my blood cells,
talking with my hands.

If you're one of the curious, press on
the candy-colored button on the glass.
Observe me either meditate or delegate
an urgent task to a future version of myself.

You can pull the viewer down further.
Watch me sleep for twelve hours at a time,
dead to the world in my large intestine.
Or catch a glimpse of me upon waking,
starring blank, describing a dream
as if in the presence of an attentive scribe.

It must be mentioned, however, what is just below
the unsung wildness of the feet.
Take note of the artist's request on the tiny brass plaque,
or security will surely remind you—
"Please do not disturb."

The Romantic

It looks better in film.
In real life, I can't see it.
I believe in it, like the blindfolded
still able to recall the brilliance of certain flowers, but
there is no sure place for it to be found.

And when it does come through, two lemon yellow empty seats
on a ferry boat—I have met so many runaways,
armfuls of candy fruits, synthetic berries in baskets.

You can sense it in the nose, this scent of a certain kind.
A persistent perfumed word turned ballroom balloon,
daisy chained to a memory—and promptly,
without hardly a savoring moment able to pass,
there it goes, gone with the dew.

Add to cart

All Things Effervesce

The bumblebee landed on the open page.
I kept shifting, waving it away as I read.
It carried on retreating, then returning.
I'm convinced it is hungry like I am hungry.

Happy Birthday

"I don't love what we've done with the place."
I say this each year when I consider it,
what it is I am to do with Earth time.

Me being me, perennially, among the ever-
expanding asphalt and metal, choking out the trees,
just a little worse, a little more coarse than the last
living day I saw before.

Not to reference natural forces
of art or of love, but out there?
If we must have billboards, make them blank
in protest for the necessity of less.
In all my lives, I've never seen such mighty garbage,
such a lack of beauty pumped and left in piles behind the eyes.

It's grown too bright; LED light
bounces off simulated things
without care, gargoyles
or handcraft.

We've all seen a patch of cheerful poppies
get the landlord special—
painted over like decorated doorknobs in a rental—
as the time for awareness has passed and yet
the bar falls lower.

What is made in haste for quick fortune
leaches into water and wind.
Artless structures come from anti-human minds.
He who has a stronghold on hope, standing in a strip mall,
has got a bit more of something than I.

Scientists say the planet is spinning faster

Tumbleweeds, When Rent Is Due

Dizzy ongoing,
holding myself up, nauseous beside doorways,
kicking bottle caps in alleyways, off-kilter
in the streets I don't need to visit again.

I can go without the faces I've seen before,
the whispers I've heard.
I can pass all the windows I've lived beyond
without looking in.
Release myself of self-betrayal
and detach from stories I told just once.

I don't need the thrills of yesterday.
The performance can end.
The song can play and then stop forever.

No pebbles, no strings.
I won't pick up these things.
The unrevealed glyphs can remain a secret.

I don't want to plant the seeds for spring.
The path is long—I knew this young, and still
so often ill-prepared for a storm so repeating.

The way I understand it,
this dry, burnt toast and empty glass arrangement—
is that all that is life, this sturdy tune and mess
(a headless laugh in a gray pinstripe suit)—
it can't have always been like this.

But for hours and sometimes days, here and there
I feel it all, simple and small—
the long and blinding walk alone.

Shadow Puppet

A monstrosity, this half-human, half-bird of whistling winds.
Snapped twig and its feathers of fallen leaves
came down, snatching through the open window after dusk.

The swift-robber, the doer for the mighty thunderer,
massive, the fanatic moral beast,
came to scoop me, drag me from the window,
not to underworld, but what lies beneath.

There was no ignoring as it shook and swayed,
surveilled, its mere presence a call to action,
though it did not act.

Each dark night, I'm left wary, off hinge.
It preys on me in memory, triggered
by any stirring, self-reflecting, involuntary flinch—
and by no surprise to me, by moonglow in the dark,
through gusts and boughs, the claw from the window
still rests on my chest.

The observed

The observer

Signs

Tossed a can in the bin,
jumped right out.

Spit a cherry pit into a bowl,
bounced onto the table.

Heard an unusual word,
the same one five times today,

and I can't keep from catching my sleeve
on the door.

Snagged by a star string, I hear it whisper,
"Don't let this go."

A repeating sequence of numbers

The Real Umbra

She is a patient spy.
An informant robed in dark matter,
but of course, you too.

The correspondence on the desk,
she read it as you wrote it.
The crony of the contract, she's always near.
Wind in the coattails, facing opposite the dawn.
The stickler, the dutiful presser.
She knows all plans laid forth,
all deeds complete and undone.

She is a quick-ticking clock.
The reviewer, the ruminator.
She waits for you—the person who waits,
the outsider, the hider—
until she knows it's time.

A lit match at your back, cigarette joining her lips—
"Give it up," moans the tall, dense mimic.
"There is nowhere to run."

Does your shadow have a name?

Cold

The light now looks different, outside idle and empty,
shone from a foreign source,
a ring-around-the-rosie with different planets,
a dull bulb from a distant, different sun.

The house, encased, drifted across space,
someplace I can only try to comprehend,
where the mourning doves are down to one
humming a dirge I've never heard.

There are footprints in the snow, but I do not recognize them.
In the house, I'm a veiled phantom hovering,
astray in a covering, tripped on a wire in a wormhole
and *poof!* I am someone else

who lives here, head full of split rail,
lonely hoarfrost sprouting through it, rooms
filled of a stranger's things.

Listless, abandoned,
there's an open book in the sink,
leaves in a tiny tornado on the stove,
a fairy ring of spoons on the floor.

I'll look again, but I'm pretty sure
the sofa has floated to the ceiling.

An ordinary wormhole

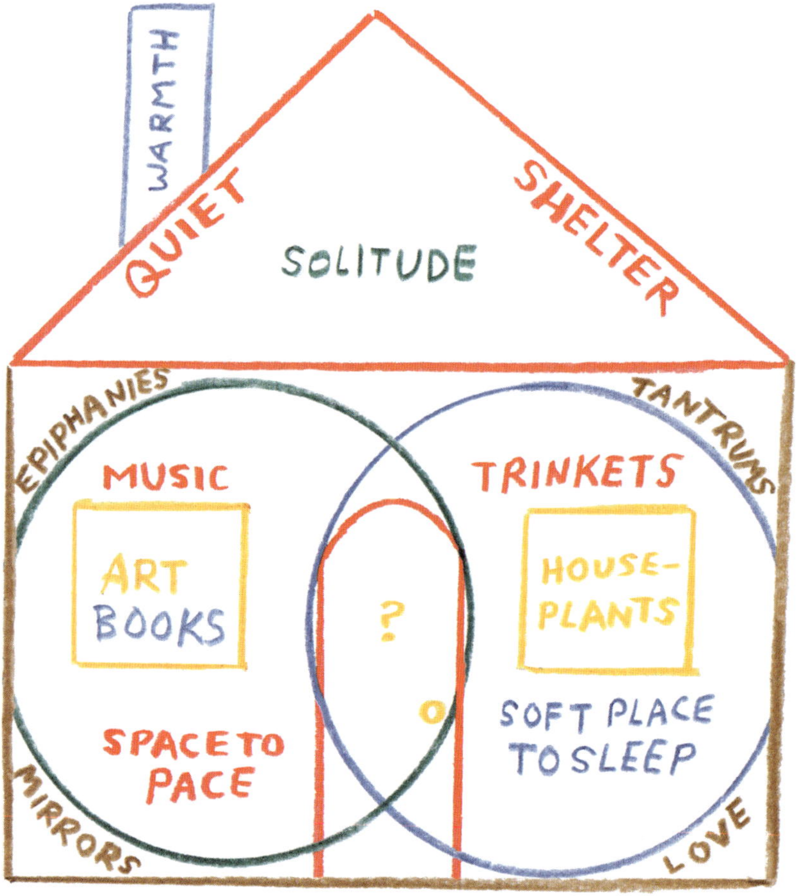

An above-average alembic

Wintering

Let the water drip.
Keep the heat alive in the house.
Drive slow, walk slow.
When it snows, remember
it is the time of year
when it can be hard to see the road,
and we must rely on our other senses
to tell us where to go.

A Dreamer Waits for Pluto

At night, I am in the hospital,
the kind for spirits of humans who can't
get it right, can't feel it right.

I turn up, or turn myself in.
Leave my belongings in the bin.
Wander the corridors in a nightgown that isn't mine.

Look through doorways a little sideways—
I am not the only drifter in need, waiting.
An IV drips, my chart hangs by the phone on the wall.

Each night we come, each night we go.
"Tear the band off your wrist,"
I heard one of them say, "No one can stay."

The Institute of Botanical Psychology and Sound

"Please try to be happy," chirped the daisy, lifting its head on a tray of brushed steel. In white coat, tape recorder in hand, trembling, the botanist cried for a year.

It's All Conjecture

Heard a theory:
Only ten percent of our soul is who we are
in body, on Earth,
the rest of us off doing things, moving
more from the seat of the spirit, in other dimensions,
wise as the whole of multitudes.

Thought of this the morning I woke up downy.
An old hologram come closer to full physical form,
I could have sworn after the dream of you,
that if this theory were true, I knew
the whole of me here—for the dream
and the fleeting mother of pearl around it—
had been bumped to twenty percent.

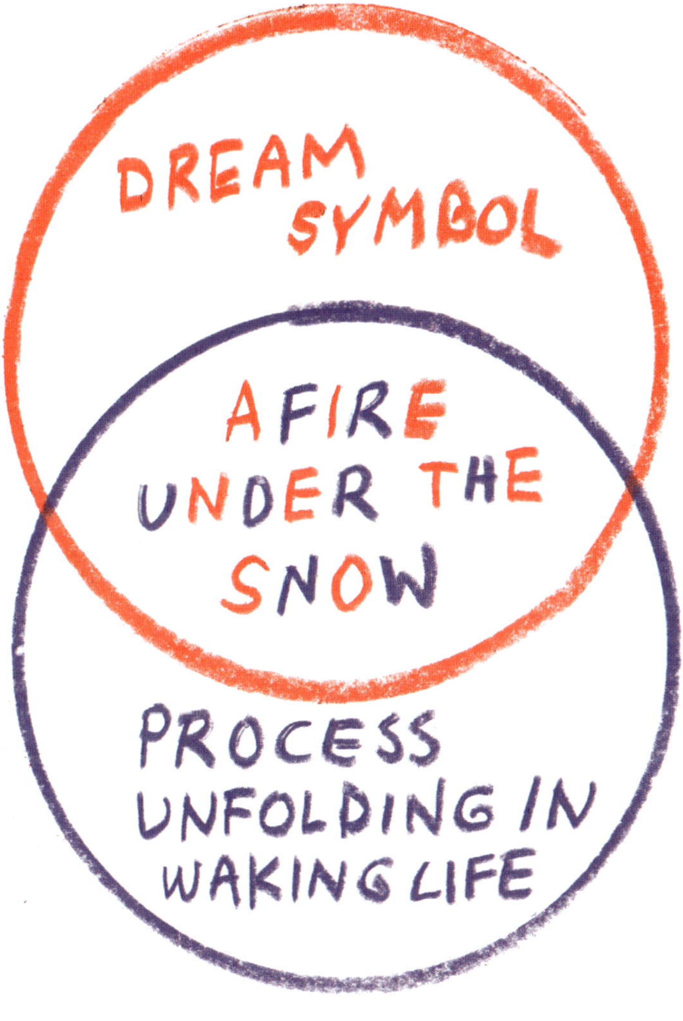

Diagram of an obvious clue

Is that all there is?

The Minotaur Invited to Dinner

I had a bowl and wooden spoon in hand,
but there wasn't much time.
A kitchen clean, which took hours,
would be no more, and alas, my horns
are buffed, my hooves are clipped and clean too,
but my mother made sure to teach me
that a guest must always bring a gift.

Oh! I know! I'll clip the flowering quince
from my backyard as a centerpiece.
Its leafed, craggy boughs could be nice.
And, well now let me take a second look.
The frost has led them unsturdy
and unlovely; this won't work.

I suppose then I can hunt in the front yard
for the tree with the least leaves,
with the berries that look like cherries,
and I'll clip them into the shape of a bouquet,
but not without ten pricks to the thumbs
and one sore middle finger, of course
from the spears I had no idea until this day
covered the berry tree.

Maybe I'll wrap them in a red hand towel and thread,
offer a warning to the host,

"Do not squeeze for danger of bloodshed."

Oh, what an obvious gift from me.
Offer something nice but that could end up
being somewhat of a problem, as if
I wasn't already concerned with concealing
my tongue just as razor keen—
a whole other thing to worry about at the table.

What a great idea, bring my own uninvited guest,
much like me, something seemingly pleasant
but sharp-edged, a thing to handle lightly,
bearing a note of caution, a phrase you'll have to
repeat
to remind people as you pass the potatoes—
"Watch out for that thing."

Temporal Table Blessing

May the softness last. May we
never lose and remember, but live in the knowing
that this all has an end—that the brute and the bleak
days and nights, by present law of Earth must turn
yellow and green, among other signs of life
from other seasons I can only faintly remember
tenderly or otherwise, on days like this.

Moiré Pattern

It is the monotony
of familiar sounds in a pattern
that never held any novelty.

The repeating shout of a car alarm.
A faucet dripping.
A baby crying through the wall.

If this sound could be a smell
it would be of your hands
after handling chains.

What is this for?
Where is the value?
When will this sound different?
When will I arrive?
"It is all not enough," I say out loud
over and over, just like the car alarm.

I am the dog
barking at itself in the mirror.

I am the baby, the broken faucet,
the links of steel and the scent of it—
the monotony.

An expiring mantra

Saint Punishing

Today I dug a hole in the yard,
sweat mixing with the dirt in the cracks
of my hands, under the awnings of my nails.
At once, when a mound was made
of earth and worms and bugs of all kinds,
I got into the hole, lay arms at my sides.
I looked up to find a stray cat looking down
at me, the mortal playing death.
A bird flew overhead and looked at the cat.
A bucket splashed nearby; a door shut.
I got up, climbed out of the hole,
walked to the back door of the house,
steam having collected on all the glass
from something come to a boil inside.

There are four hundred and ninety-nine

TO FREE

"Hello, this is the unknown speaking—"

The New Year Kisses Right on the Mouth

It is January 1st, and I am googling caskets.
"Oh, that one is reaaaaally nice," I catch myself saying
under my breath, as if window shopping
out-of-budget winter scarves.

It is January 1st; and I am googling caskets, or rather now
the difference between those and a coffin.
"The coffin is more humble, yes, that's more me—"
I catch myself again, knowing a box burial never felt right.

It is January 1st; I have claustrophobia, and I am googling caskets.
"Quilted satin lining. Too fancy—and slippery."
"White linen on the inside. That's classic," I say with my chest
when I come across a modest wicker coffin, and I am
thrilled to find something timeless and biodegradable.

I am on board.
I nickname the box The Hamper,
read how it's suited for both straight to burial or cremation,
and I begin to wonder how quickly you would need to hold service
to be in the basket prior to cremation,
without the requirement of being embalmed.

It is January 1st, and I am googling caskets,
getting caught up in the logistics of spoilage,
like calculating the wiseness of consuming leftovers,
and wondering why I, a maximalist,
appear to be drawn toward a minimalist end.

Free calendar with purchase

Potential past lives

A Friend's Mom Called Me Wild Once

I would have liked to tumble right into this life
the untethered, real wild animal.
An alpine woodland sprite of instinct and fur
of this whirling, drumming world. Just existing
with streams of unbroken silence, and what breaks it,
merely shaken off. Powered by an unconditional love
called Curiosity and Presence, but not as we know it—
uncomplicated and eternally fresh of a life
only under the light of sun, moon, and star. So charged
by the earth, naked paws at home in the dirt,
not this constricting, frenzied seesaw,
overkneaded global imbroglio,
long human story of learning to unlearn,
born of false barriers and our subconscious,
uproarious arguments with them,
when I could have held onto it from the start—
the receiving, a letting in of the composite
spectrum of light as it bathes, day after day,
and I, feeling it, sustaining it,
long enough it's in the marrow,
which by vibration blends with the soul.
A creature of burrow and moss (*take me there now?*),
I'd only see the details of myself in the ripples
of the occasional pond and puddle.
No overthinking or other reasons for howling,
save for noble warding, and love, and play—
like a tired, tattered, velveteen being
come bright-eyed and alive,
befriending squirrels and bugs, tucked away
far from all our roads and hunters,
up high in the thick
of the sidereal spirit of the mountains.

The Difficulty of Being

Where my soul stands in my human
there is a banana peel.
Or is it—
there is a banana peel in my soul
where my human stands?

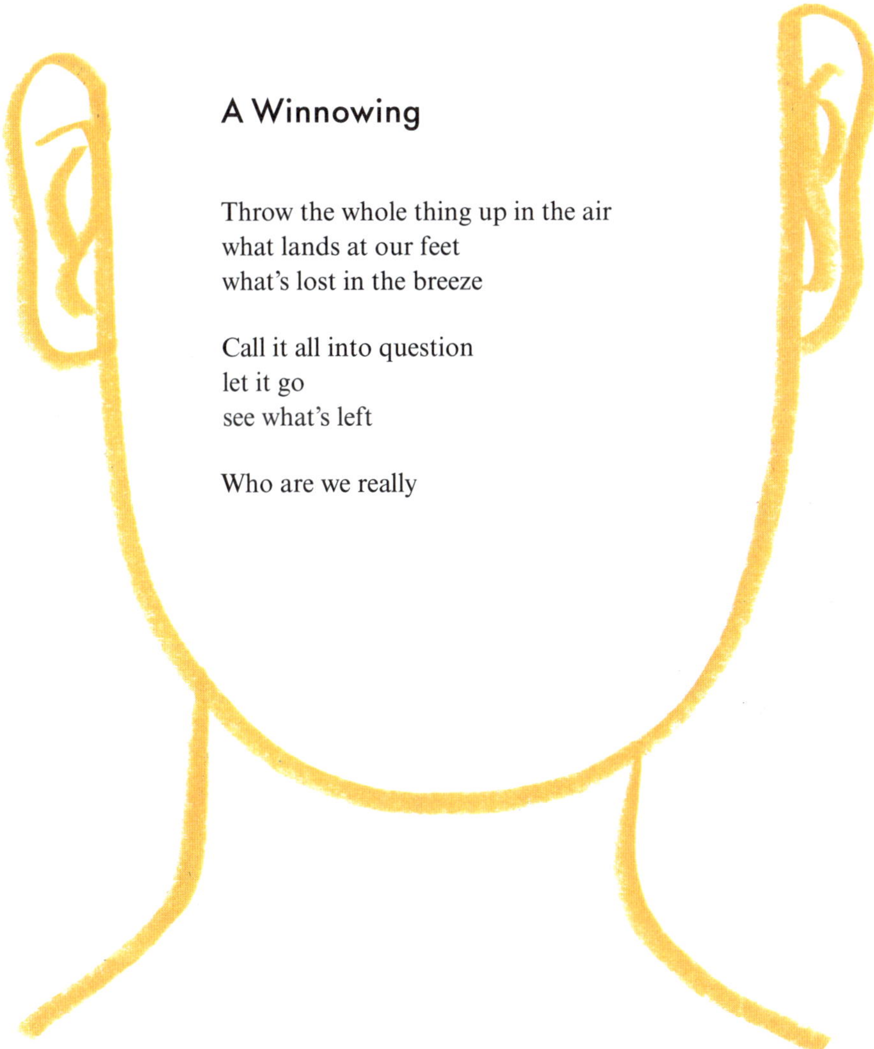

A Winnowing

Throw the whole thing up in the air
what lands at our feet
what's lost in the breeze

Call it all into question
let it go
see what's left

Who are we really

Yarn scraps, or

a result of synaptic pruning

We Are Haunted Houses

Smoldering embers, what had burned already
had not burned enough, tough and still breaking
apart—this was a resuming fire.

Inside, multiples of me, self-combusting, igniting
the house, snaps and pops, soon orange roar.
Dramatic reenactment, or is it prophecy?

The pyrotechnic at the center; the obscured conductor;
magician striking baton in violent jerks; orchestrating
cinders; high and low; vigorous, informing flames

where to go, here, there, above, underneath.
What is easily lit goes easily quick—
retro patterns in presentation and belief, the obsolete.

What has dried in the sun is what burns, heats,
turns to nothingness, blown by tall whirls of fire self-possessed,
exposing what's left standing,

just the conductor, just one of me.

In Defense of Strangeness

If there was
no great heaping
haunting, lurking
tap-dancing mystery—
would there be any fire
in the mind at all?

Bedside stack

Hour of Parting

I am too busy in this small life
of many lives, being quiet,
washing the corpse of who I was
with cloth and bucket, reviewing
the lines in the skin, watching
for the eyelashes to flutter, sighing
repeatedly, looking at myself in the face
while gently combing my hair

Climbing smoke, human hair, or a wave about to break

Something to Say at Any Point in Time

This charming grave.
This sacred life.
What am I doing here?

A FAMILY
OF DEER FEED
ON ROSEHIPS
SOAKED IN
A LUNAR GLOW
WHILE I SLEEP
FIVE FEET AWAY
DREAMING OF
LIVES I'VE NEVER
KNOWN

A country tableau

Like a Shepherd Moon

There is a kind of love
as a learner, I'd call it a more-love
I have only known it from the Other Place

Round
Whole
Huge

A meditative magic with no tricks

A myth
A carrot
A promise

I realized after attempting to consciously conjure it—
if dreams are any clue of death,
I have no problem with living and dying at all

What will we ever do about tomorrow?

Sixteen Tons

The average choice has become the trap.
Have kinder conclusions crawled into the heart
like a couple of mice? Or bird friends
sewing, tying bows right where you toil?
A little lipstick on an unpaid gig or low wage,
when all you want is a world to be free
and leave what it does not need.
And leaving is a privilege, and of great cost.

The modern mind is trained to work as a generator
of future proportions, stretching outward,
and so how do you stop projecting the images
of somewhere else, and exist and enjoy
without taking note of next steps, having to be—
for the sole purpose that you must be—
on the move, on the cut, and do?
Let's get through all these bills without dying.

We throw it around, neuroticism.
Devalue our uniqueness, dismissed natural states
that should be playing, offering and receiving
care, enriching community, but instead, confined
in the label of false safety, security beneath a mask
of conformity, and even the word ME in all caps.

If basic needs were set, maybe then
there'd be time for choosing and resting
in choice, to be as we are, as we continue to change,
without brand, rush, or repurpose of capability,
to exploit our timeless being, and those of others
just to keep bound to the beast for another day.
"Life is suffering."
Yes—I am asking why.

Cartoon money

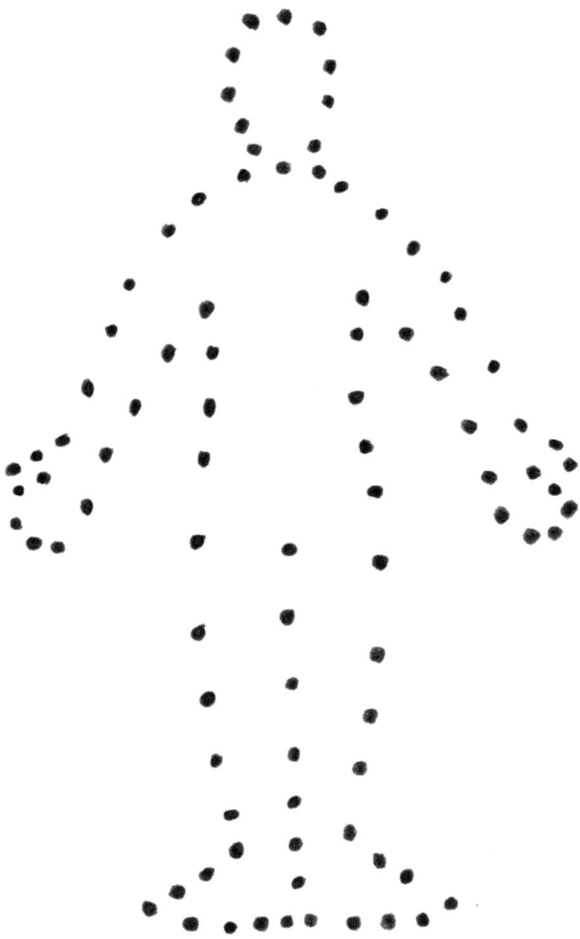

Connecting the dots at the grocery store

Public Services Needed

I haven't found the breathing machines.
I have come from another place where they're all over.
There should be one here in the center of the transit station,
another beside the candy kiosk at the shopping mall.
Outside the courthouse there should be a whole row,
and also, rather generally, one should always know
in any borough where to find one.

We need to see the opportunity,
like a snack in a coin-operated appliance
that requires no coin.
Across the top of the breathing machine
in bright hand-painted script it should read,
"You can have this, it is safe."
"This, my dear, is for you."

Separating Melody from Accompaniment

One must wonder—
the one who swears they're at the edge of life
or just about where the pages should end,
the one who sees sidelong without newness,
drifting about, done with dance and free from desire,
cleans their home in silence just to wait
in it the same, hands folded neatly in the lap,
burned their spirit over coals
of industry, no longer soul in body
but a specter, a protector of the mundane,
calloused and thick, lost all ability to feel
the full figure of living or even just the gift
of absolute relief from being alive that comes
from time to time in a full body laugh—
one might begin to wonder then,
if over many lives, they had seen it all.

I know I haven't seen it all,
some days though I believe I've seen enough.
But as it kicks and gallops,
here I am still, amid the bucking,
legs wrapped around the ride.

For even now as I hear a cross-country train
far off, late at night, through the walls of my room,
I have a thought that feels like the truth—
a recollecting
that at some cosmic impasse, countless lives ago,
I made a choice to live inside a story.

Yeehaw, I guess

Headphones

I am no airshow or firework person.
I prefer the mystery along the creek.
The suspicious, quiet, satellite watching sky.
Panels projected onto our second set of eyes.
The crowdless long way, the scenic drive.
Times where there is no sense of time.
The focused experiment, registering the depths of hue.
This must be the cause of misophonia too.
Counting the layers—how deep does the thicket go?
Had I ever been awake this time of day in spring?
Foraging for featherlight perceptions—
before a tremendous blast or terrific pounding roar,
there is no room for me.

Ode to a Nap

Outside of time
all rough edges
are smooth

A Brief and Holy Nothing

Flooding the plants, the rain
on the roof, pooling in the dip in the deck,
reminds me of nothing.
The stars overhead are laying off the jokes
for once.
The barberry and the pansies are getting watered,
the windows washed.
A mess collecting on the steps.
All I can smell is the water in the dirt.
Light keeps changing, clouds strobe the room
gold and warm to cold and grey.
The house doesn't care.

Things carry on,
lying in the window, waiting for no one.
My body just a body.
My head just a head.

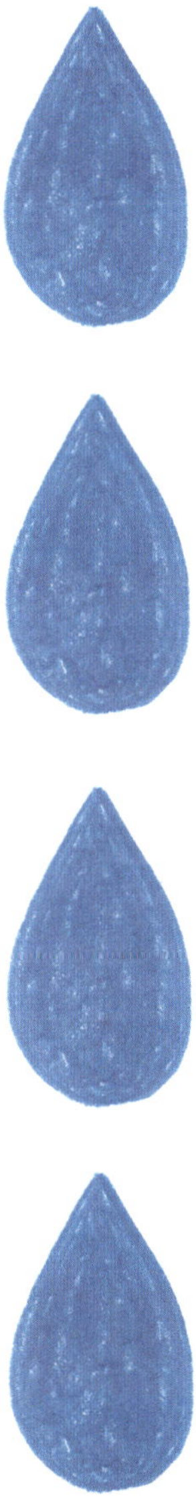

Wheel of Fortune

If sunlight passes through
raindrops at just the right angle
and if there is an observer,
light is split into an arc of colors.

What is your sunlight
What is your rain drops
What are you here to birth

Every rainbow is a circle,
it also works in reverse—
the other half in muted shades
upside down through the earth.

For Better or for Worse

Mirrors are everywhere, but they don't really do it.
A gallery of photos of every time you rounded off
a jagged edge—how would it change you?

Your Own Heart Says

Show me
the red in your cheeks
without pinching

Witness

A whale bursts upward
from the wide-open door of the ocean
and returns.

*

It's worth noting, sometimes
good things may pop into view
just to show us they exist.

The Hidden Treasures Are for the Diver

There is a tide pool in the middle of the human body,
liquid collecting from the eyes and the mind
and the soul—can you hear it? The tideland,

the concealed crystalline surf
as it sings, warbles and glugs,
its gravity tugging knots tied intricate
and to your center—can you feel it?

Water trickles soft, back and then forth.
Can you see it? The changing tide
where crab legs hide behind anemone,

gulfweed and tangle, sea star and galaxy of limpet.
And closer, bright sharp marine salt that opens the face,
chambers awakened, too, in the lungs.

Watch as the moon-snail befriends the nudibranch
throbbing on the red velvet sponge.
See between orange tongue, the trumpet worm tickle the sculpin,
a flirtation ongoing from the beginning of time.

Slipper moss and streamers of green,
heart cockle and striped butter clam,
pink mouths in plumes and spikes of the urchin burst—
they decorate the water table,
that birthday song and intercession,
this place to light candles.

The shallow teaches that to begin to know it is to allow
the noise outside the body to recede,
to direct your sodden eyes right at it.
Fear not your reflection in the sea,
nor the jellyfish, the octo', the eel—
when you're ready, channel the turnstone,
break the water-wall face first.

Packing list for the deep

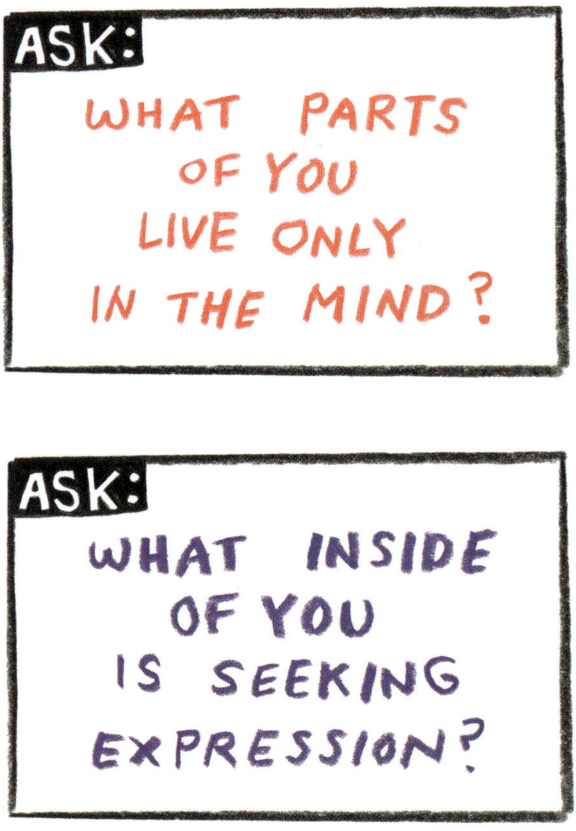

Instructions for an exorcism

Bird Chorus

The early-bird part of the self, the sleep-severed hunk
only alert when I wake at the break of dawn—
in certain strident chirps, in text italicized and bold—
this bird of me declares that I have never enjoyed every poem
of a single poet, every film of the filmmaker,
every song from the band.

Another bird, perched within me, whispers in cursive,
"These kinds of wounds heal quicker in the sun."

Outside are branches snapping, the country buck
rubbing antlers, grunting, hooves crunching leaves.
Inside, I pause in front of the painting—
the ship at sail, the speared whale—I stare,
neurons scrambling. *How to affix the birds' words*
with the chewing gum of a passing strength of will?

With the force of a life of wishing,
I begin the stitching.

Sunday Paper

Our mothers scream when we are born,
a reminder from the start we are not casually alive.
We come by flood, as seen through human time
on Earth, leave our mark, a body lived
in the same collective dream.

Left fingerprints on gold-leafed baroque doors
like the hands that looted Nefertari's tomb.
Toss notes for each other in bottles in the ocean,
blueprints for how to live full and fight strong.
Blood, plaques, and paperwork
to produce, procure, and defend our imprints.
Built statues in memoriam for revolving faces
of questionable statesmen and world changers.
Crafted arrowhead and bowl, buried deep across continents—
remember what we wore then.
Passed down how to cook it best—pig bone and rhubarb pie.
When to hang the garlands and what it means.
Where to bathe the forest and why—
desire paths teaching us how things should have been.
Hands fondle unlacquered cast brass
through eras that make it shine everlasting.
Each insect we encounter, part of us knows the lesson—
fear and how we strike it—a tethered tale to tell.
Our mistreatments through the lineage, too, don't forget,
also sweetened with experiences of devotion, tenderness.

Though space junk and our secondary dreams clog the ether
and bounce through our technology of air—
have you ever listened to the snow as it falls,
how it cloak-silences all of it? Mom once taught me
how to hold a rabbit. My arms and hands have never forgotten—
that could be a clue. Though I trust to walk the maze-dream
honest, a bare minimum,
is to announce as it applies at breakfast,
"I am also in it hemorrhaging—
in and out of love with it, too."

Emergency Alert Poem

You are a part of all that is
which is to say, even
amid transition and delay,
you are whole as is.
You are a happening
within the happening.

An adventure within an adventure

Field Notes

The back aches to no surprise of the ego
or the spirit, in the hesitations of being alive
in a way that feels most genuine
after consecutive epochs of puppet showing
and bending for the dollar.

We can only free it now moving forward and inward.
There seems now no way to go up
without showing the way down.
No moving forward even a step
without hatching inward.
No getting out without first getting in.

Having trudged around, goofed about,
found some shortcut to the door—
it's true, once you see it,
it is the only way through.

TO
IMBUE

Glimpses

Woke from a dream to see a calm
speckled fawn lying on the rug
in my room
Its ears twitched
I woke up again
to find my pillow and blanket on the floor
in the exact soft shape of the fawn

Gotta Get Up

Ascend into daylight
Prying open a coffin made of pine
makes the same sound, or
the knotted reverb of weeds
being yanked from the dirt by the roots, or
pulling a muscle in the legs,
megaphone at the tendon—the sound
brings the blood around the bones

STEP 1:
PICK THE HONEYSUCKLE
STEP 2:
PINCH THE END OF THE FLOWER AND SLOWLY PULL THE PETALS FROM THE STEM
STEP 3:
LICK THE NECTAR FROM THE STEM

How to do it

The Danse Macabre

The mouth of life opened with cypress trees.
Four San Francisco blocks from the Pacific
and the dunes, there stood two cypress statues
at the entrance to my childhood house.

Here, time passed in dead goldfish,
as our family would bury them below the cypresses
underneath red bricks as grave markers in the dirt.

When we weren't building burials,
my brother and I, kissed by the beach,
would pick seed cones from the cypress branches,
roll them in our hands to smell them,
and throw them at each other.

After bouts of solitary tempests of the spirit,
years later, my brother would be forced
to leave this world for the next one,
and I would learn in classical antiquity
that the cypress was a symbol of death,
immortality, mourning,
a staple of the cemetery.

I've begun to think, myself
an unremitting, flicked playing card
in the spokes of the years of my life—
that the older and stranger we get, the more saturated,
early and obvious the themes.
Consider in theatre, if you pay attention
to the production from the opening,
you can grow an ear for the underground,
returning melodies throughout, hinted from the overture.

As a kid, once asleep, I swam in night terrors,
human bodies buried in the backyard, rising from the dead.
As an adult, preoccupied with the afterlife—
its numerous and most numinous forms—
I've dug deep, looking for the leitmotif.

Was it the terrible dreams—
grey arms out before them,
those corpses from the garden that sat up straight?
The goldfish, in their shoebox plots out front?
Or was it that archetypal double face of Janus,
an innate trait on the prowl,
or that bigger-than-the biggest collective
unconscious howl of the cypresses?

I also have wondered if a part of me had known
from doing all of this in another life maybe once before—
that loss, by universal law, carries a trick.
It can, under certain constellations, produce a gateway,
a heavy pour of primordial light into
life. For at its most fundamental, a death
of any kind, with its myriad polar manifestations,
is a doorway—for the griever and the grieved—
a threshold between rooms.

Dollhouse

They recommend to lucid dream—
if you've got an interest and would like the advice—
to try to remember in dream moments to look at your hands.
Also, it is suggested to open a window if it's closed,
walk through a doorway if you see one,
flick the lights off and on if you come across a switch.

There is a sort of liberating glitch that can occur
when the mind can remember to look for such things
and can manage to adjust something small on the astral plane.
How odd, to unlock our ghost from a sleep within a sleep,
we do simple everyday awake things to claim our agency.

The next time I find myself spinning off my top, or
having lived a string of too many days all melted into one,
I will try to remember to look at my hands.
At night, my house will be the one seen from the street
with the lights strobing on and then off and then on.

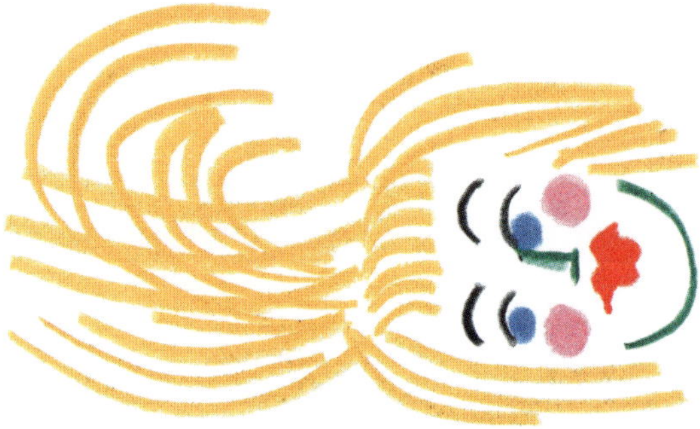

A Manta Ray Driving a Car

Woke up with gills all over me, slits, breathing
open and close like Argus, but instead of blinking eyes,
one hundred moist half-moons

This all over mouth and breath, I am made now
to exist in more realms than one
and thus, appear strange on several plains

Down in the brine, though the wailing still exists,
tears can't be seen when one cries, underwater
one does not need legs for walking either, but I have them

And there, though with gills, I still have two human lungs,
vestigial, like my knowledge of spreadsheets
in the waters of the deep

There still, sea friends speak to me in convex tones,
and make a little fun of the shape of my nose
and the design of my feet

Up here, blushing, breathing on everything,
one of my gills sighed in the mirror
and blew out a candle with my elbow

And when flanked by the saints, Garlic and Onion,
and if I eat them—comic-strip stink lines,
how they come from everywhere

On land, to keep friends, I've the pain now of limiting alliums,
and seeking new clothes to better suit how I breathe—
a looser gather, wide eyelets

The whole stretch will have to be custom, but I'm not angry,
I never liked thick socks, tight jeans, or turtlenecks,
and I can say overall I do breathe better

Art Direction for the Portrait Photographer

I intend to be myself, true and earnest.
To look at life square, without faking,
the way the serious people look
in the earliest films and photographs—
of steel, a tad ghastly.

Think of the Victorians, stone-faced, collar up to the chin,
eagerly awaiting sundown and seance.
Or long before, the early depictions of Medusa,
her eyes and those of the snakes staring forward,
having kept more secrets than you.

Oh, to be as open in the eyes
as the ancient votives of Mesopotamia,
looking at eternity, attentive and wide—
not waiting, but perpetually seeing.

We mustn't forget either to capture, even momentarily,
the folktale wolf of me, leering, mouth open,
pleased with how sharp my teeth have become.

It is perhaps my highest goal today
to let my spirit slip out my eyes just the same—
cold in presentation, maybe,
but built of hot blood, and a certainty.

Backup plans

SPIDER ~~Simon~~ Says

You have to stay slick.
Say, "So long, I am not your true target,"
to the figures that shout and suggest you stay still—
the constraints, the convention, the prattle,
sometimes the loudest voice inside yourself.

You must stay on high watch for what adheres.
Practice the chant, "Be gone with you!"
in the direction of the village voices
that roam and demand you must change whole shape
for their own incurious comfort—
stiff, latched, claiming you can't arrive
as you are, you can't be odd, a little off,
unsuspecting, or new.

The side we like to hide cannot be eaten like a secret.
We cannot swallow the unlit half with the gilded throat.
Time skips along holding hands with the volcano, and you as well
won't be able to keep it down—this inevitable purge.

Those not yet at the same mark in the path
may have you thinking this is a geyser of regret
to be concealed, but you'll beam.
You'll have got this all out, your body
knowing just what to do with it,
as the self, if eaten to be hidden, is no fuel
nor food of pleasure, but a poison.

Following your guttural oust, this rejection
from devouring what cannot be kept down,
exhausted and proud, you'll simply wipe your wet mouth
and smile, or even better—don't.

This must be acknowledged, this truth,
this little bit of strangeness, this umbrous energy,
this sense of humor just sometimes like broken glass.

Please keep in mind, like brushing your teeth
or looking both ways before crossing the street,
that to be disliked by some is an effect of being known—
that it can be wonderful to be the weird one,
a bit steeped in cypher,
and to sometimes feel akin to the unfavored spider,
making plans for winged things on a bed it made for itself—
happily alone, and misunderstood.

By sun or by moon, find north by shadows

Re: Your Request

I'm sorry.
Respectfully, I cannot commit to the project.
Last night I dreamed a bird flew out of my left eye,
telling me this is not the way.
Should you reach out at a later date
with something new for me to do,
I will ask the bird again.

Mise en Abyme

If past lives and future lives
are parallel, lives happening all at once—
time only present construct, not overruling infinite order—
then a healing in one life, in one body,
is a kind of healing in all, which is to say,
when we act in full possession of ourselves,
question the blame, embody the change,
we shall certainly feel the wind blowing in our hair

Imagine, a room full of mirrors,
you, never ending, incarnations—
and when something is transmuted, which is the cure,
we are all released, a double-beat miracle in the breast,
our hearts across planes, a palpitation
feeling as though it has come from nowhere

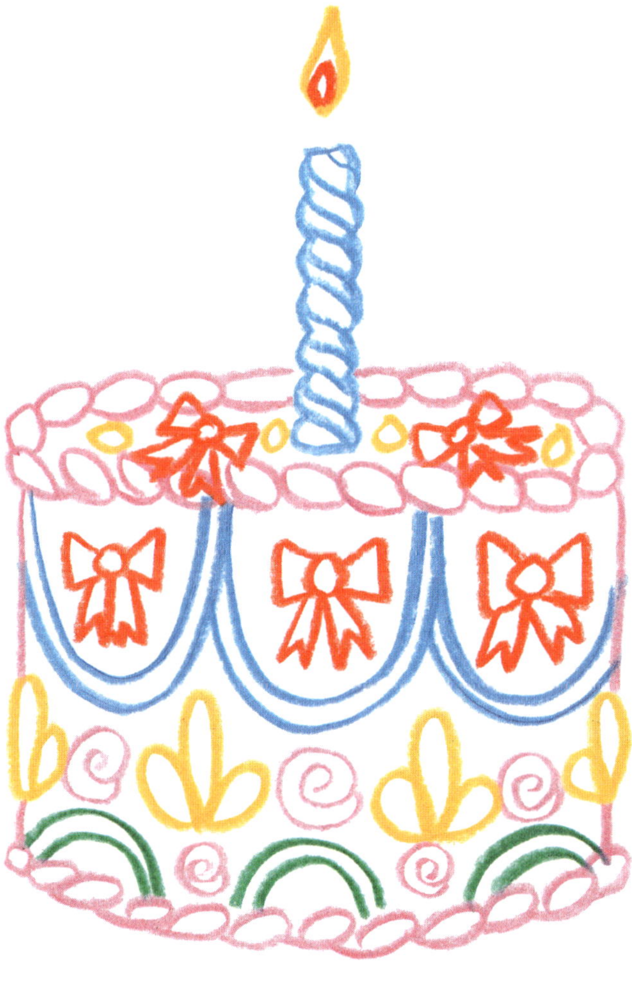

Cake for no reason

By and By Anyway

All that can dazzle in the miracle, of our world,
of light and condensed matter, exists within.
Things of solid form and optic beauty
are but ritual
props to remind us and each other
who we are.
And props are meant for the temporary
and some don't seem to need them at all.
And who am I
to say that we shouldn't let either side of this coin
be hot in the pocket.
Beneath a laminated virtue,
it is the human thing.
Despite the hand-to-hand pamphlets,
the revolving door of popular culture—
to go through life and not make it out
clean or alive?
My dear friend, it is not cringe to die.
There is no cringe body in this world,
for even the hateful fool is deserving
of a different expression.

Beware the Bezold Effect

Remember to maintain your own kaleidoscopic experience of waking.
One filmstrip without cuts—a solid thing, an ensemble continuous—
as is the being, though coiffed and cleaned however million times.

Because we must, we garnish ourselves for the carousel, but
don't let the world, the day, tell you what year it is, or how to think
of your vessel in a space muted by industrial, occupied time.

Let us have all of our coffees and teas in touch with our ageless
energy—
the you who observes without words, moves without moving,
loves without having received love, forever has a treat to eat
in the heart, for there is always something shining there.

In the evening, when the sky burns alive, for the sake of all
that came before and still what may, don't assume it's all like the rest.
Know that it is you who decides. It is you who tells the time. It is you.

A knowable magic

The Jeweler at Lunch

Why does the past
and the future seem broad,
but the present a dying spark?
What is a moment measured?
Why is a moment larger in the mind
in the past than in the future?
What if the present moment was as vast as the past
and the future feels?
Rather than a small bead of possibility
sitting on a string strung long in both directions,
what about a bead the size of it all?

21st-Century Awe

Big death cherry at the center, portentous orb
of the evening gleams, punch-up peach and navel orange,
just before it's painted over blueberry bloom.
It's honeyed fingers through the leaves in the elder trees,
process again through the window.
The Venetian blinds are a gobo,
suggest bibliomancy, gold dust in thin glint streaks,
highlighting sentences in a book
between my hands.

It came to me as gentle strips, a projection
from the camera obscura, upside-down
and reversed from the lake—molten sun glade
blinking into and out of existence like quantum foam;
waves in lines, through an unknown trillions of miles,
filters of rock and gas from space, ozone
on through the multitudinous veils of Earth-nature.
Colored by wildfire—this brilliance, a small apology
from a natural response of an unnatural disaster.

The screen on the window and the slow-clearing smoke
in the air, they add to its visual density,
the result of a convoluted journey,
working harder than I in this exact moment
to be this shape and shade of light.

Giant

Is the sound a cricket makes any business of the cricket?
The vibrations of a rock tumbling down a mountain,
does it care? Are we serious
imagining we are not the rock, not the cricket—
but the wizard? Despite a lack of proof
that the cricket and the rock don't feel the same.
We sleep and wake at a dawn.
The rock warms in daylight, as does the cricket.
I am not certain they both don't consider the sun the self.

Drawing a Diagram on a Chalkboard

A circle walker and a half-circle walker.
Either way of moving can't be wrong.
Unless the half-circle walker attempts to disqualify
the full-circle walker for claiming to circle it
when they themselves have only witnessed the walking of the half.
Or, if the full-circle walker claims the circle
in its entirety is the only walk worth walking.
Not to mention those that walk the circle must know
surely, that there are more than just one.

It's beginning to make simple sense
as we are, as I understand it, everything
and all of us, one big walker walking—
that all walkers will eventually get to where they need
to walk. In time and for the sake of relaxing
some historic tension, I think you'll find
it is best if we eat our fingers pointed
towards how the others talk of walking
and instead decide to walk and talk.

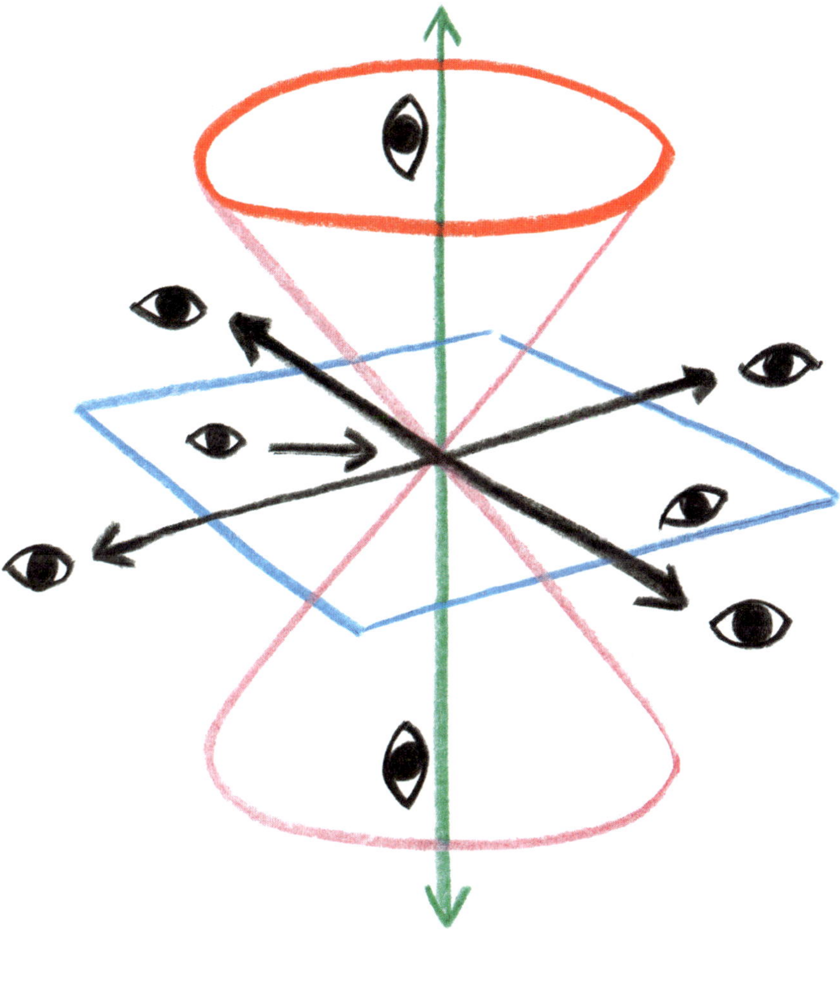

Spacetime of One (simplified)

Premonition Dream

I saw a sunrise before it happened.
I knew it, the day opening on a beach.
Though the idea of light was coming
oddly from the north, gilding the thoughts
of those gathering down by the shore,
it lit nothing else—
rocks and cove and bodies
still blue from midnight.

A party at high tide, I was up,
way up top along the cliff, gazing down
at their puffed ruddy cheeks, watching proud.
Smiling, I whispered to someone standing east,
"The sun has already come upon the beach."

A dawning, the temperament of driftwood over flame—
the ecstatic crowd along the cove danced
in the sunrise that hadn't happened yet,
their spirits the size of a round golden ghost
along a cool morning coast
gradually becoming
something both deathless and entirely new.

The Third Eye Can Open Wider

It is there for you to grasp.
A pooling satori, a soft thrum.
A movie outside of time, in the periphery—
the unmeasurable, unfilmable, abstract moving images;
the synesthete's colors for a precog transmission,
like that of a cactus knowing it will flower
long before it ever could.

I can't tell you exactly how one receives it,
it does not lend itself to simple terms,
but imagine the eurythmic consciousness
of a network from prehistory, ancient
though unnamed and without signs of age—
often subtle, like the rustling of a goldfinch
in a thicket, in a quiet part of the mind.

To spot it, you might see a flash
of the colored subterranean quartzes that speak
vast, like fungi that carry messages
(which we all know are secrets).
You might hear metamorphic rocks,
their boop-bops and beep-zings—
impressions a person might receive,
headfirst, listening for it,
wedged among the drip-drops
in a cavern, in a hole.

There, I believe you can find it
at its most round.

An Odd Delicacy

Sleep adventures in the waking hour.
Sweaty palms and secret horror.
Is there a crack in consciousness?
Exhausted, reading a book
or tiring over the day in a chair—
an audible orchestra, a bronze blast of images begin,
not in the room but between the ears, a musical
excess of evaporating lightning.

Have you read the invitation,
the playful, benevolent call?
The surrealists knew it, employed it
to puncture the linking mortar wall
of sleep and dream,
the state most betwixt, most known,
between the in-between and the tangible.

So is the visit from the phoenix, as a flicker.
Diana in the pasture with bow and cimaruta, and then gone.
The lit circus tent seen from afar in a field
and by a warp speed appearing right before you.
Then, a curtain opening,
a gloved hand waving you in,
and falling, falling, falling.

Hypnagogia—like all creative features,
a slice of the experience of being,
the unconscious mind—a projector
that has not a split, but an aperture,
a leak of light,
not a losing, but taking the lead,
the film rolling, the dream
beginning to play.

Each a haunting surprise

A Ghost Dressed Up Like a Person Dressed Up Like a Ghost

Me and my ghost smile at each other
as we begin to sing the same moss-covered song.
I had ordinarily been better at singing the low notes.
My ghost also struggled hitting it high, but now
we look at each other, sing through the laugh,
giggle through disharmonic cracks.
This is how we are—lunchpail love notes,
its chin on my shoulder as we drive over the ice,
identical holes in our identical shrouds.
It stands watching by the punch bowl
as all past versions of me fling our bodies
in sunbursts, under bunting and bright lights.

The Whistler Knows

To strive to be a wind instrument,
or rather, to be one, and keep trying to be it.
To meet what was lost, or
what it has opened, to observe them
from several angles in different light,
at various times of the day, as you grow
to see what has been blown into your side—
this constellation of cavities.

To try without trying, to listen.
The wind can blow through them
if you let yourself listen, that is
if you come into the privilege of quiet moments
and apply to the wounds a patient focus—
from these hollows there are songs.

Living Water

An inner truth is a conductive entity.
Its contours and resonance, how it calls to us,
edits and grows, moment by moment
as new data electrifies faster than the speed of light.

We are never the exact same as we were the moment before—
so is the natural world, all that surrounds,
whether or not we accept or perceive it—
it is the right time all the time to change.

To honor it is to live as expressions of it.
Not a fixed thing, but another mysterious,
ever-moving, ever-growing thing,
like a plant that sprouted from seed
through the earth, all of its gestures, casts,
a representation of something real.

Contraction, Then

Pathways unfold.
Things occur to you.
Flowers appear out of thin air.

Flour Sack Prints and Dandelion Salad

The crone in a cotton dress
picking flowers along a meadow
somewhere—I would like to say
someday, before my bow,
that I ate the whole apple, stem and core,
and threw out nothing

For the occasion of being alive

A way of seeing

A Vision of a Better World Is Not a Mirage

Upon waking from the dream,
there may be seasons the act of walking
can jostle the aura enough to detach.
You can even attempt to dislodge by leaping
into distraction, work or screen, or both—
though the dream is a microorganism,
likes to live, kindly and potent,
not just in the aura, but the bones—
and if you are not careful, the tenderness can pass
right through the barrier of the brain.

It sees itself in the water in the body, and bonds.
Hitchhikes on the backs of blood cells,
goes tubing down the rapids of the legs,
paddles back up the sparkling stream of the spine.
You really should be careful, unless you are vigilant
and keep busy for busy sake; otherwise
it is beyond all intellectual doubt—
your days will be colored by the dream.

It will take your eyeballs, turn them
into a set of pinwheels, heart-shaped buoys,
and fingers crossed with the normal things. Go ahead,
try to write your name without a chromatic circle in mind
or a hillside of French court jester marigolds.
Good luck maintaining a grip on the false edge of anything;
you will only be running your fingers over petals,
hands through the water break.
You will feel once and then again and again
that curiosity is the way.

Inherent Psychedelia

Leaving the womb,
the first learned wound. The sun
gives life, too, and burns.

It's all archways, archways,
and more archways, endlessly
entering the room after endlessly leaving it,
by collapsing, the body let go,
transformed into table flowers, rainwater.

But the other self, of weightless stuff
one might see as light
that bounces off silver and gold—
it never leaves anywhere,
just expands to hold more.

A polyonymous thing

You and the Mystery

When you start
listening more to the Mystery,
the Mystery starts
listening more to you.
It is a conversation,
like the kind that happens between
a particular flower in a garden and its admirer; it knows
that you are looking. The Mystery is excited
when you are excited because of course
you and the Mystery are just two different names
for the same thing.

EYES OPEN

HEART OPEN

REMEMBER?

Remember?

Hermes in a party hat

As Above, So Below

The arm fell off, the dead weight come off the body.
A guy had to come to saw it in half to take it away.
Two other people came in an uproar of sawdust
to trim more of the arms, leaving raw amber
stumps aglow, to keep
another substantial arm from the prospect of falling, too.
And now I've got to tell you about the doubt.

I have spent years sitting beneath this earthly body
on a wooden deck in my late grandmother's chair, observing
the crawl, encroaching, closing in of the deck,
as the canopy grew longer and larger, from the grass
over the wood, softly touching the house.

I couldn't see as much of the ether as I could before.
From spring blossom to summer, the fruit of the body
weighted the arms and kept them hanging low. I did not realize
as the space around the body in the yard was not wide enough,
did not allow enough distance for me to see how it was growing—
the width of the body obfuscating the height.

Autumn and winter, too, the body made a cage of the outdoors
and oh, how I felt without consciously acknowledging—hemmed in
—and although I can appreciate dapple and how its lace adds romance
to any calloused, wood-splintered hand, and how
on sun-scorched days the body's shade did bring regular relief—
do not even get me started on how many shooting stars,
under cover of leaf, I may have missed.
But now, the dead body gone, the hardy body pruned,
I see it, with the charity of simple written words.

Throughout the seasons, this body and crown, now freshly cut,
was never a coop, nor a ceiling that I had been beneath
but rather before, a burgeoning body
that lives half an unseen atmosphere.

I am not the person anymore who ponders why
driving through the redwood forests of California feels like flying
through a sun-told heirophany.
I could argue even the sapling in any state
is a kind of multiradial devi.

A murmuration beneath the leaves has become plenty
in the body, on this earth. I'm convinced
when what constricts is released from its ties, when action is taken
to remove excess, and one is willing to look
with all our eyes, we see distinctly
the actual height in a given space,
its potential to house a tower,
and we receive the staggering gift—a clear view
of the body already grown tall.

The Space Between Two Things Is a Portal

People, hands
Eyes, trees
Cats, doors
Lands, streams

Skills, thoughts
States, dreams

Cracks,
and all else
you can imagine

Archetype Parade

We all pass through the myths, the arches,
largely not at all noting with regularity their charge
and that we are, in a way, participating
in a small symbolic rite, coming and going,
the potential for renewal as we travel between them.

Everything we do can be seen to be saturated
with meaning. A transformative force,
the currents of such individual meaning, haunting,
coinciding with what preexisted, yet is still dancing
a multidimensional ritual.

Even without our knowledge or conscious decree,
this illuminated manuscript—
a deep, meticulous craft interwoven
of the past—it is claiming us right back,
and we are always in its company.

Across dream, thought, materiality, when they slip into view—
it is equivalent to echolocation as a solid,
or learning that upon leaving a bottle of wine on a grave,
that this did actually mean the dead, festooned,
could lift it to their lips without end
and drink from it.

The room is never empty

The Ebbinghaus Illusion

Small and also large.
Ruler and also pauper.
A summer melon and a meat.
No one knows why, but,
"Kid, be grateful," they say,
"This is yours."

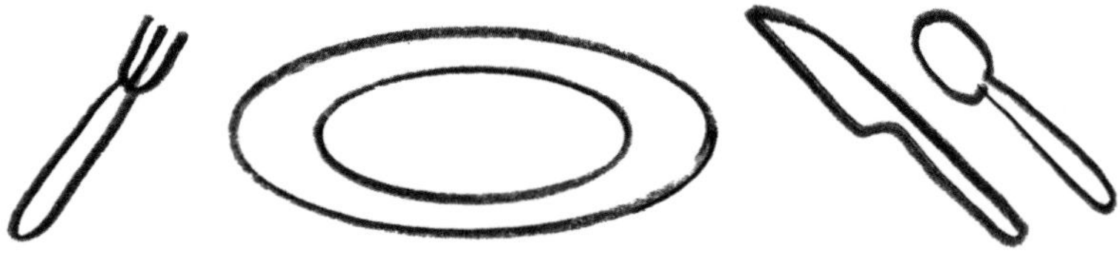

Shouting Guidance in Reverse

Episodes underground, seen in rearview,
are like having spotted a dear friend
slipping, arms flailing, legs whipping around,
trying to stay steady on compacted snow.
Look at that absolute human being—walk slower!
Take your time!
Breathe and reassess!
But no, they must keep bending, contorting,
shoe-gliding, muscle-pulling.
A rubber man in an earthquake.
The windsock man in a storm.

Use the Big Fire

to light the little fires;
keep the candle lit in the chest.
Log who comes around to blow it out.

Stay inquiring, handy.
Spare a light for the neighbor
when you see a candle dim or disappear,
and if all you've got is your breath,
let that be the summoner,
what whips a glow back into flame.

If it is our own torch that cools, gets doused,
or if our hands can't feel a thing
where our brightness should be,

plainly do your best
not to wait for someone else
to notice, to burn for you.

Seek fresh ignitions and get
comfortable asking for a favor.

Something new begins by our beginning

The Temporary Is the Sacred

If you're uninspired, splintered,
two of you become opposites—
the first, driving a bicycle through the dirt,
the second, dragging by a chain behind it—
your subconscious and its arrangement
with unconscious rest may decide,
in a desperate attempt to decompartmentalize,
to call on the spirit of a Wise One.

They'll sit with you on a curb to commiserate
near the drain where all your confidence pooled.
They're here because you're here, at the precipice,
having forgotten all your incantations.

Things that wrap this catastrophe in a bow,
mirroring your movements, kicking rocks,
they'll share insights your conscious mind may not remember,
though in the morning, through the astral steam,
in the missing puzzle piece reflections and themes,
you'll sense them at work, heart rinsed and rung
having remembered how you were lifted,
absolved of weight and wall in the in-between—
the space where all that is comes together to lift.

These bellows to the fire, this is how it goes.
A movie at the cinema ends, we return
to movements we know,
half-head in a new light on the walk home,
a little more alive than before.

A list of wise ones (abridged)

The Intuition, the Wind

The sail, the sensitivity
The skipper, the spirit
The boat, the body
The water, the life

Heavy Weather Sailing

Having fallen from the sky—
the amnesia of being a thing
that had to enter time to become
something new, to be on a planet alive—
I had felt as though I had been in weighted shoes
someone else strapped me into.
I was backpacked and yelping along
the banks of an unending nonsense, though
the more I allow myself to return,
the more I let myself learn of myself,
I am certain it was me who tied these laces.
I am, to a fault, come alive by running races,
and a challenge is a challenge, is a challenge.

The spark-lights I've seen, far off
on the horizon where the lines begin to split,
I had been too scared, too frightened to tell another,
for I never saw a way to get along
living as true to it as it feels I came here to be.

But now that I hit a solid at the center, and more,
I implore all the glimmerers and glimpsers—
if you're seeing those lights, too, off in the distance,
we must begin to speak of them,
if not for all else, to see how many of us
came here, not only to catch the flashes,
but to point at them in the company of others.

Please remind me when I forget

Communitas

There is a collective harmony to be made
with the complex arias, throbbing outward and colliding,
from each of our individual torments—sing!

I sense it, without question, from the state of things.
I hear it, the chest pounding across airwaves, the static
erratic treble from the TV, the shortwave radio that plays the news.

I see it in the faces of world neighbors across states
when common disagreements fade with the loss
of the same finger, and also

oh, how we love to love when it is permitted,
but limitations in hand is the plan, local and offshore,
to cause our saltiest tears to freeze and fall behind closed doors.

I see it in the cost of everything, bread and self respect
of a realm abundant with resource, and yet
whose needs are really being met?

Expand the awareness of your orbit and beyond it.
Sleeping, eating, laughing, being held—
it's as if they want us to forget.

I feel it from all the noise blowing through us. If you haven't,
observe the sweat—to be online is to be a part-time industrial sieve,
sparking at the socket, just about to pop.

We need more, and we are remembering
that more comes from less; more of what is inherently gifted
from the earth—less machine, less force, less stolen time.

No creature only eats just to keep its face alive.
A tree is not intent on just a single wooded arm bearing fruit.
There are other ways of living we haven't considered before.

I've been possessed by it, too, the wildcat of need
to build something better with what we're given,
even if it seems sometimes like it's not in the stars.

In my atoms, I know that what must be changed
to sustain and to thrive, the birth cannot be trusted to come
from any suit or court card unfamiliar with common song.

I can smell it on the wisps of the ghosts, darting about the house.
The spirits, they pulse, as parts of our one choral, polyphonic whole,
"We are you, and you are us, or else how could you sense it?"

With the wisdom of the gut, I understand it like dominoes,
how they are flicked, click, and fall. The human voice, cracking,
even a ballad long gone carries the urge to join chords.

Tempo

To succeed is to catch up to the rhythm of a thing.
You cannot turn the page of newsprint gracefully
without the knowledge of how the paper bends.
Filling the cup without spilling requires the slow pour.
The driving, we must feel with the whole self
how the machine likes to move and how wide.
Making the bed is a quick chore when we agree
with how different weights of cloth fall in the air.

Finding your footing on a ship at sea.
How to angle the oars in the water.
How to channel the strength on empty—
we learn the rhythm by trying.

Thresholds in waiting

Clay

I have heard the old ranchers say
over compost and dead-heading,
that a June petal drop from the fruit trees is perfect for a wedding.

In charity shops drowning in antique linens,
I have heard it said while reminiscing,
that a sheet of winter ice is ripe for cold-water fishing.

We can't forget the quest, despite chaos and bargaining—
that we must walk light, as Huxley wrote,
and do a little something with all this everything.

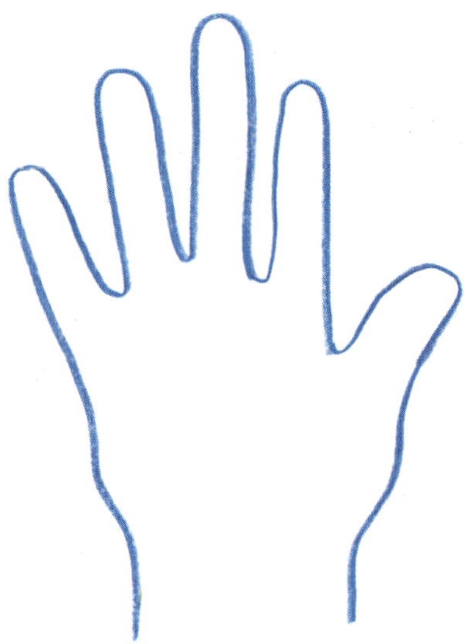

Afterword

I've stressed on more than one occasion in this collection the importance of tuning in to one's self and one's intuition. This is by design. I find this tuning in to be fundamental to navigating life as a highly sensitive person, and particularly as an artist.

Outside of my commercial and editorial work, I have often preferred to engage in art making by creating first and determining any meaning or purpose, beyond meditative benefits, as a secondary affair. In this way, I enable myself to tune in to something seemingly more pure than my conscious mind can conjure. Call it following the intuition, communing with the unconscious, channeling, or simply entering into a flow; the liberating practice of letting creative energy move through without plan or judgement allows anyone with a typewriter or a guitar, a paintbrush or a crayon, to explore the garden of their ideas, as well as the weather that birthed them. Tuning in this way can open up new dialogues not only with the self, but with the vast unseen. It is a means of expanding the mind beyond its everyday perimeter, noticing a sort of zephyr in the reeds, and attempting to illuminate where it's coming from. I credit some the greatest pivots of my life and my favorite creative impulses to sensing and being in conversation with this kind of inner movement. A creative method like this from start to finish could be compared to entering into a waking dream, transcribing it in some way, and then analyzing it. This book came into being no differently.

The poems and drawings in this collection were developed over the course of several years after I followed this very inner movement. I felt a strong magnetic pull, and let it lead me to relocate my home and art studio from San Francisco to a sleepy, small rural town in the Pacific Northwest. Apart from the bucolic vortex in my new backyard that pumped out a steady stream of white-tailed deer and mysterious, kindly black cats—for all intents and purposes, during this time I lived alone. Visitors overall were scarce; seldom did I travel far.

I felt there was a purpose to this way of living, but I did not yet know it fully. Many of my friends and family were understandably confused by my sudden move to "the middle of nowhere," and it would take these strange years alone to understand it myself.

I wrote several hundred poems in my solitude. I drew mountains of drawings. I didn't know what I was ultimately doing or creating, but I was tapping into shuttered old places and new wide-open spaces within myself. I became a student of my own quietude and the accumulated raucous that had so long swept over it, and over these years, off on my own, I noticed myself changing. Holed up in the country in an old house—bottling myself, cooking in my own juices, for better or for worse—I had unknowingly entered into a ritual of transformation at the root. Heralded, chaperoned even, by strange synchronicities, archetypal visions in meditations, and dreams of ancient symbology (imagery I hadn't yet discovered as preexisting motifs of the human psyche)—this was my confirmation. By act of listening to my inner sensing and moving with it, I had created an ideal environment for an elaborate alchemical process. This book, at its essence, is its record.

Now, with regard to taking experimental direction in life from one's deep-feeling perceptions, I do not advocate for marooning the ego entirely or for wholly ignoring one's clear senses or basic morals in favor of an assumed, intuitive hit. I am also not an individualist. I do not assert that such profound isolation as I experienced (if you can avoid it) is necessarily something to aspire to or that it is a suitable solution to one's common problems—quite the contrary; I believe we as humans should embrace the faculties we're given and each other. Let this book be proof as well that just because you are following your spirit does not mean that all the road ahead of you will be clear and without its trials. (We are here having the human experience, after all.) I do, however, hold nature and the voice of intuition, both of which we are inherently a part, in high esteem. I trust that if we find a way to listen to our inward sound and keep our eyes open to the symbolic nature of our world, be it in our day-to-day lives or at the easel, it can help guide us along our path and bring us closer to our own unique medicine.

Eyes wide open to our uncertain world and its literal and figurative rapidly changing climate, I believe a relationship to this inner activity—its resulting sharpened sense of discernment, as well as its life-giving qualities—is more important than ever.

Dear reader, not only do I hope that this book brought you entertainment and a sense that you are not walking the coals of this life alone, but my sincerest hope, above all else, is that this work might assist in fortifying your connection to the natural world, our shared mystery, and your own creative inner guidance. In other words, if you were at all in need, I hope you, too, found something to transform.

Notes

To Burn, To Free, To Imbue

Chapter titles are inspired by the stages of alchemy outlined in various alchemical texts of the ancients, mirrored most notably in the last century in *Psychology and Alchemy,* and other various works by Carl Jung. Though the chapter titles carry the essences of these varying stages of alchemy, they have been truncated and renamed to reflect the unique meander of the individual within the structure of the alchemical process.

The Difficulty of Being

Title is borrowed from *The Difficulty of Being* by Jean Cocteau.

Hour of Parting

Title is borrowed from the jazz standard "Hour of Parting," specifically the spirit of the version recorded by Sun Ra.

Wheel of Fortune

The third to the last line is influenced by the poem "Dream Dust" by Langston Hughes.

Beware the Bezold Effect

Title is in reference to an optical illusion discovered by Wilhelm von Bezold, where a color may appear different depending upon the other colors that surround it.

Spacetime of One (simplified)

Illustration is inspired by the light cones commonly used to depict Minkowski spacetime, developed by mathematician Hermann Minkowski.

Living Water

Title is a nod to *Água Viva* by Clarice Lispector.

As Above, So Below

Title is borrowed from the popular paraphrase of the second line in the ancient text *The Emerald Tablet*, attributed to Hermes Trismegistus.

The Ebbinghaus Illusion

Title is in reference to an optical illusion discovered by Hermann Ebbinghaus, in which the perception of the size of a circle can be distorted depending upon the size of other circles that surround it.

The Temporary Is the Sacred

Poem title is borrowed from a line in the poem, "On a New Year's Eve" by June Jordan.

Communitas

Title is borrowed from anthropologist Victor Turner and his concept of communitas, outlined in *The Ritual Process: Structure and Anti-Structure*.

Clay

The second to last line is in reference to a quote from *Island* by Aldous Huxley.

Index

Acknowledgments

To my literary agent, Kelly Bergh (The Magician): Like most things that appear fated and serendipitous, you came along out of nowhere and at the exact right time. Thank you for your enthusiasm, your crucial guidance, your ongoing support, and your hard work. I am beyond grateful.

To my editors: Molly Ahuja, one million thank yous for believing in me and my book, and for advocating for it—it's hard to imagine things getting off the ground without you. Kara Knickerbocker, thank you for your eye, your playful suggestions, as well as your ax.

To Ann Barton, William Thomas, and the rest of the team at DK and Penguin Random House: Thank you for your trust, your structure and flexibility, and your continued support.

To my book designer, Chelsea Bianchini: Thank you for your wonderful attitude, your ideas, and your great work throughout the process. It's been a delight to come together again.

To everyone cited in my notes section: I am in your debt. Thank you for your contributions to the world.

To my past collaborators, my clients and patrons—creative and spiritual, online and in the flesh: Your place alongside me on my path has been so far significant, and I have never taken your support for granted. Thank you.

To Alan Black: Thank you for your creative writing guidance. You read some of my poems long before anyone should have, and I thank you for being open and encouraging.

To my friends and family: I can't believe I get to know each of you. Thank you for keeping me company these last several years, primarily over phone and video call. Without you, being away would have been something very different. Mom, Catherine, Jim, Christine, thank you for your love and unwavering support. Dash, Dad, Paul, Grandma, Grandpa, along with the rest of the family in spirit, thank you for the continued visits and for being in my ear—it is one of my most favorite things.

To the wildlife and abundant nature of Oregon: Thank you for always looking back at me, and straight in the eye.

About the Author

Katie Benn is an artist and writer from San Francisco currently living in southern Oregon. Inspired by all things mysterious, dreamy, and absurd, she explores themes relating to the human condition and her inner world. Katie works in various mediums and has exhibited her artwork in galleries across the globe. Her editorial illustrations can be found in publications such as *Bon Appétit, Condé Nast Traveler, Frankie Magazine, Food & Wine, Wired Japan, MIT Technology Review, McSweeney's Illustoria Magazine, Süddeutsche Zeitung, Los Angeles Magazine,* and more. In addition to her creative work, Katie is also a psychic medium offering a down-to-earth and heart-focused approach to connecting individuals with their loved ones in spirit.

@katie_benn_ | www.katiebenn.com

RULE OF THE GAME:
TRY TO DO SOMETHING ABOUT IT